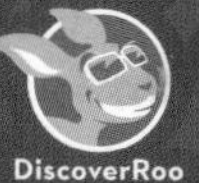

An Imprint of Pop!
popbooksonline.com

Historical Biographies

VINCENT VAN GOGH

Post-Impressionist Painter

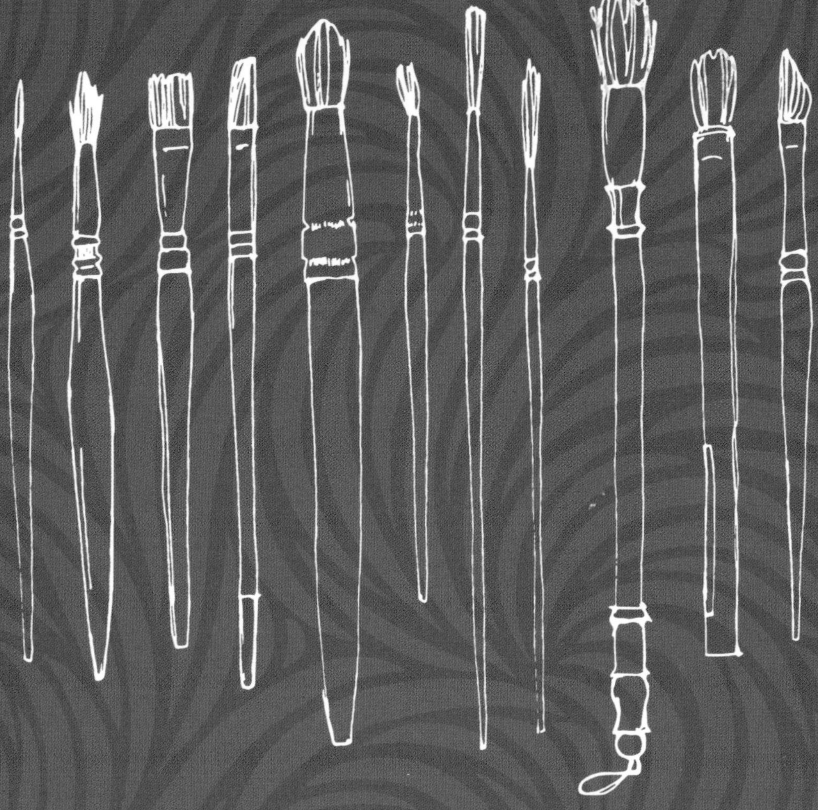

by Grace Hansen

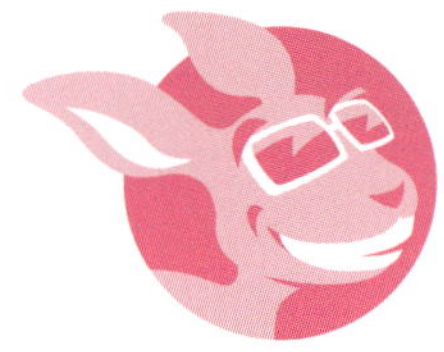

WELCOME TO DiscoverRoo!

This book is filled with videos, puzzles, games, and more! Scan the QR codes* while you read, or visit the website below to make this book pop.

popbooksonline.com/van-gogh

abdobooks.com

Published by Pop!, a division of ABDO, PO Box 398166, Minneapolis, Minnesota 55439.

Printed in the United States of America, North Mankato, Minnesota.

102022
012023

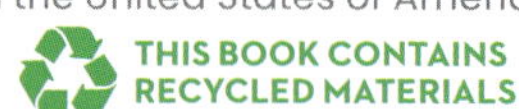

Cover Photo: *Vincent van Gogh* by John Peter Russell (1858-1930)

Interior Photos: Shutterstock Images; Alamy; Getty Images; *Portrait of Vincent van Gogh* by Henri de Toulouse-Lautrec (1864-1901)

Editor: Elizabeth Andrews

Series Designers: Laura Graphenteen; Neil Klinepier

Library of Congress Control Number: 2022941243

Publisher's Cataloging-in-Publication Data

Names: Hansen, Grace, author.

Title: Vincent van Gogh: post-impressionist painter / by Grace Hansen

Description: Minneapolis, Minnesota : Pop!, 2023 | Series: Historical biographies | Includes online resources and index.

Identifiers: ISBN 9781098243432 (lib. bdg.) | ISBN 9781098244132 (ebook)

Subjects: LCSH: Gogh, Vincent van, 1853-1890--Juvenile literature. | Painters--Biography--Juvenile literature. | Artists--Biography--Juvenile literature. | Postimpressionism (Art)--Juvenile literature. | Portraitists--Biography--Juvenile literature.

Classification: DDC 759.9492 [B]--dc23

*Scanning QR codes requires a web-enabled smart device with a QR code reader app and a camera.

TABLE OF CONTENTS

CHAPTER 1

PAINT WHAT YOU KNOW, VAN GOGH!

Authors often work by the saying, "Write what you know." Artist Vincent van Gogh did the same with his craft. He painted what he saw and experienced. Today, people can see this when they look at Van Gogh's work and personal letters. Though his life was often filled with

WATCH A VIDEO HERE!

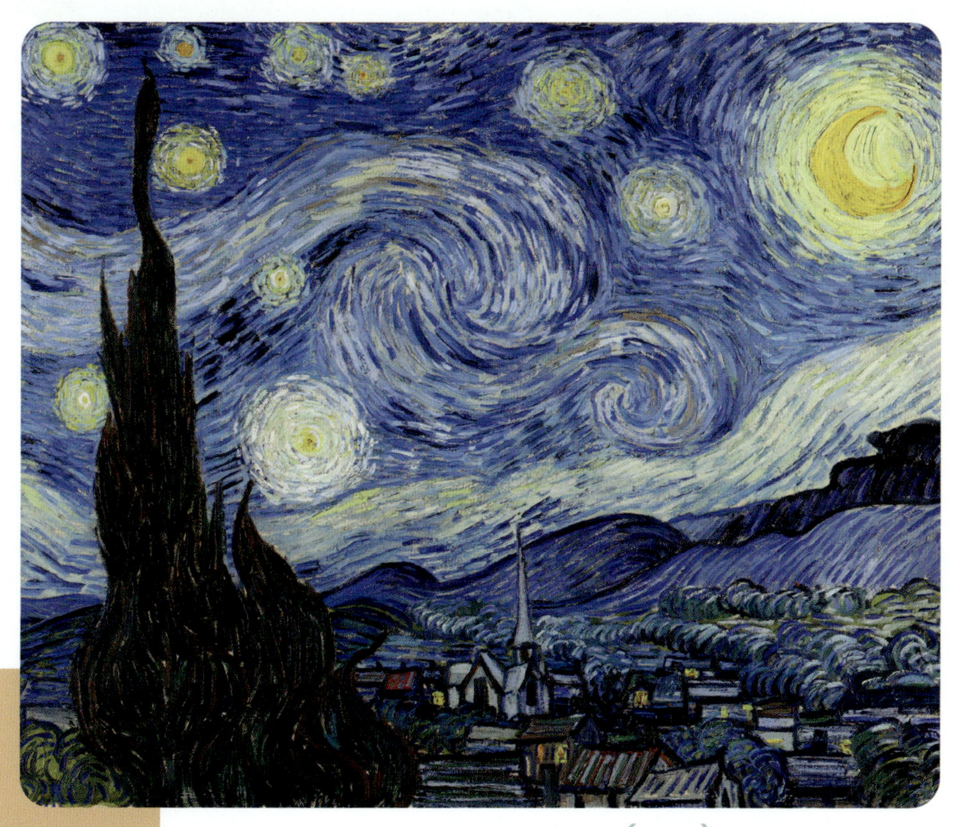

The Starry Night (1889) is one of Van Gogh's most celebrated works.

sadness and uncertainty, there were moments of peace as well. And all of it can be experienced through his hundreds of oil paintings and drawings.

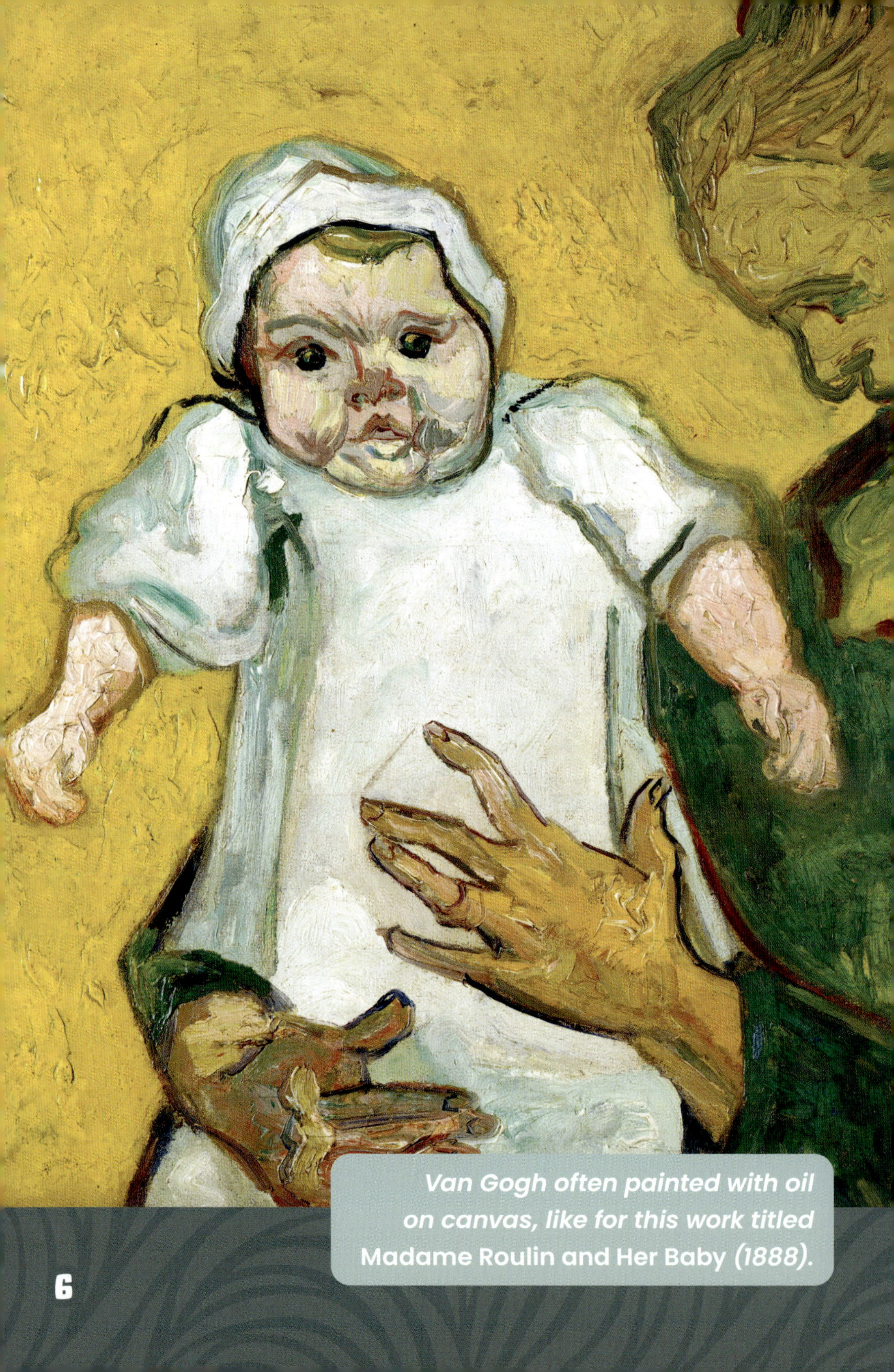

Van Gogh often painted with oil on canvas, like for this work titled Madame Roulin and Her Baby *(1888).*

Vincent Willem van Gogh was born in Zundert, the Netherlands, on March 30, 1853. His father, Theodorus van Gogh, was a pastor at a church. His mother, Anna Cornelia Carbentus, was from The Hague. This was an important **cultural** center in the Netherlands. Vincent would later spend time there **honing** his craft.

Theodorus and Anna had six children. Vincent was their eldest. He had an especially close bond with his brother Theo that would last until his death.

As a child, Vincent loved to read. He also enjoyed nature. His family often went on long walks. Vincent spent hours outside collecting insects and studying plants and animals.

When it was time to go to school, Vincent was not especially fond of it. However, he was able to study art later in his education. Since many members of his family were art dealers, the subject caught his interest.

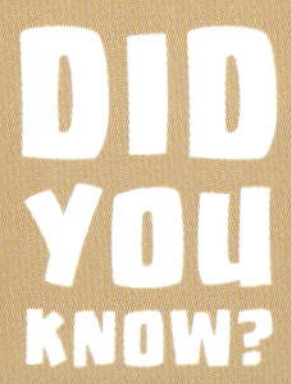

An art dealer is a person or company that buys and sells art, or acts as a link between buyers and sellers.

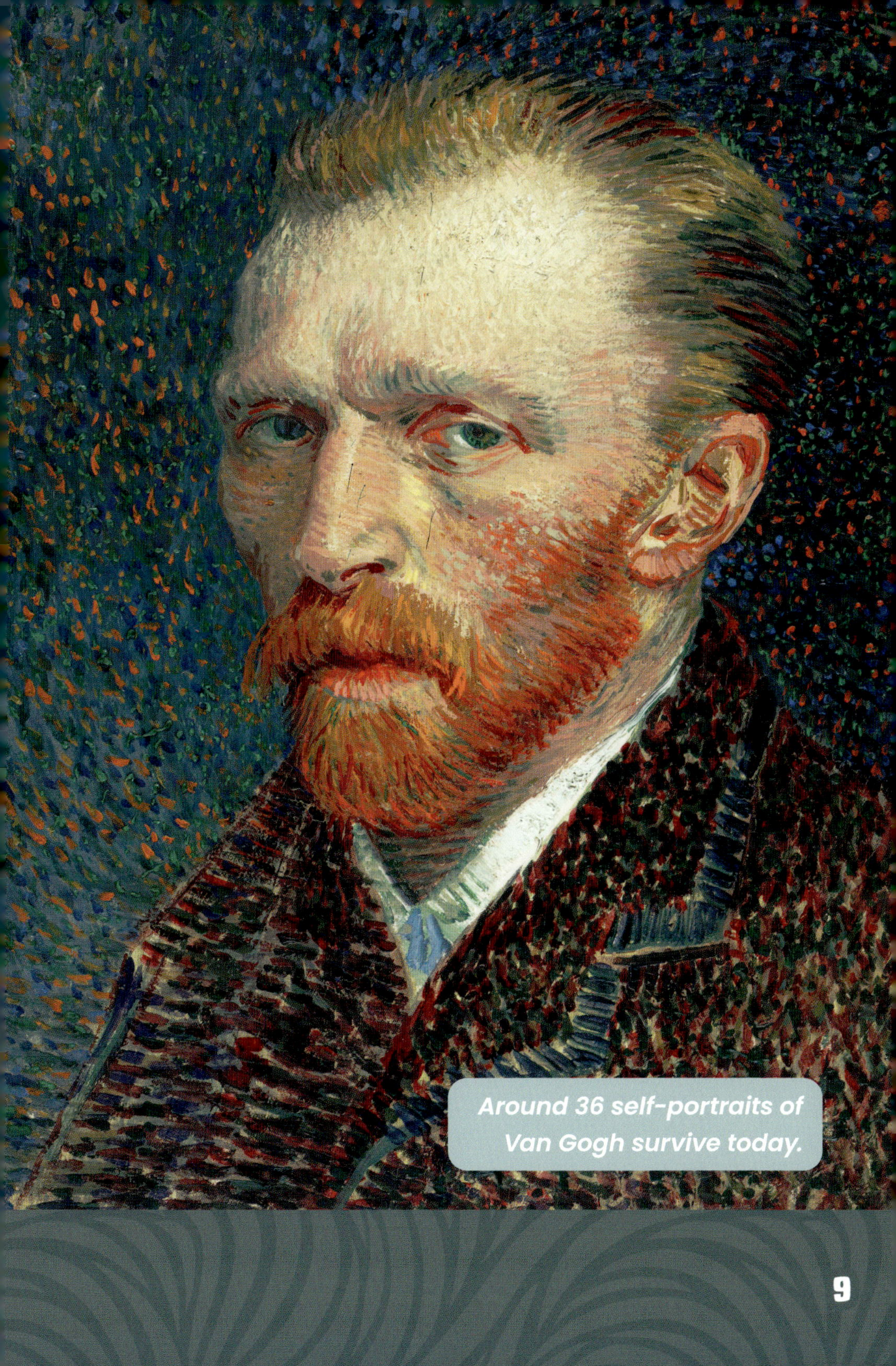

Around 36 self-portraits of Van Gogh survive today.

CHAPTER 2

ART, RELIGION, AND POTATOES

In 1869, Vincent followed in his family's footsteps. He was **apprenticed** to Goupil & Co. as an art dealer. The company had offices in several European cities. The job exposed Vincent to many places, museums, and artists, helping him appreciate art.

LEARN MORE HERE!

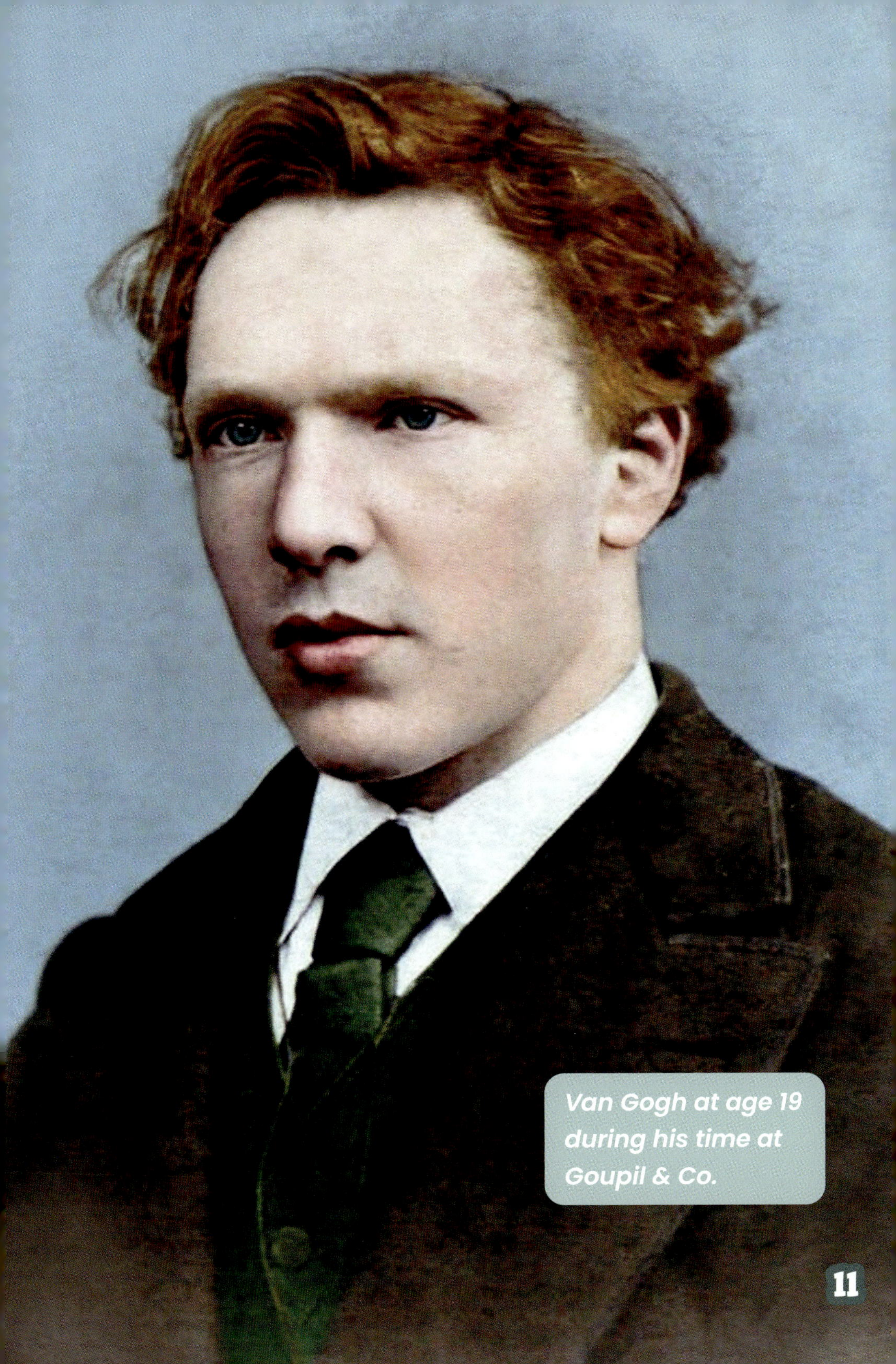

Van Gogh at age 19 during his time at Goupil & Co.

However, Vincent was not meant to be an art dealer. The company dismissed him in 1876. At the same time, he was becoming more interested in religion.

In 1878, Vincent was sent as a **missionary** to Borinage, a coal-mining region in Belgium. Life there was difficult for the **peasants**. Fewer were working in farming, and instead taking jobs in factories. The work was dangerous and paid very little.

Vincent felt sorry for the peasants of Borinage. At one point, he gave away all his possessions to help the coal miners. He slept on a dirt floor. Though he connected with the people, he failed to gather any religious followers. So, the church removed him from his post.

Van Gogh painted Still Life with Open Bible *not long after the death of his father, a pastor, in March 1885.*

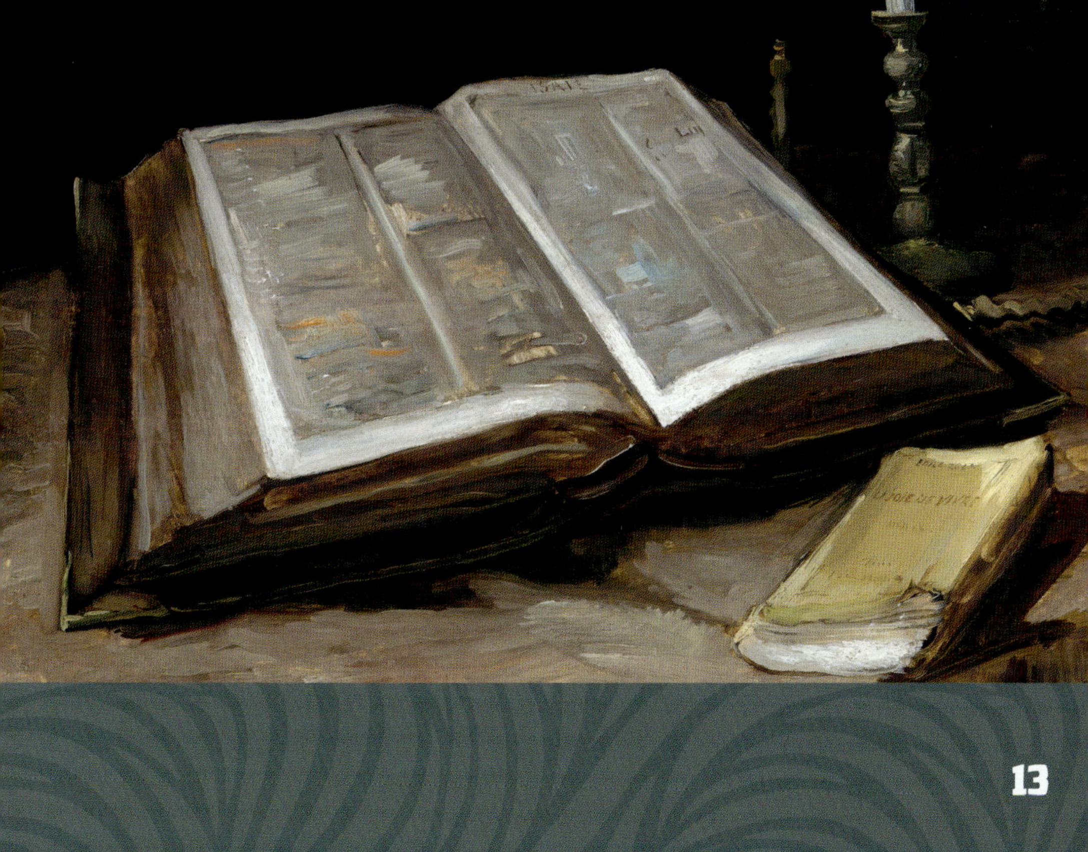

Vincent felt discouraged. He did not know who he was meant to be. But a former teacher encouraged him to stay in the town and try working with art again. So, he lived with the peasants and drew them. His confidence began to grow.

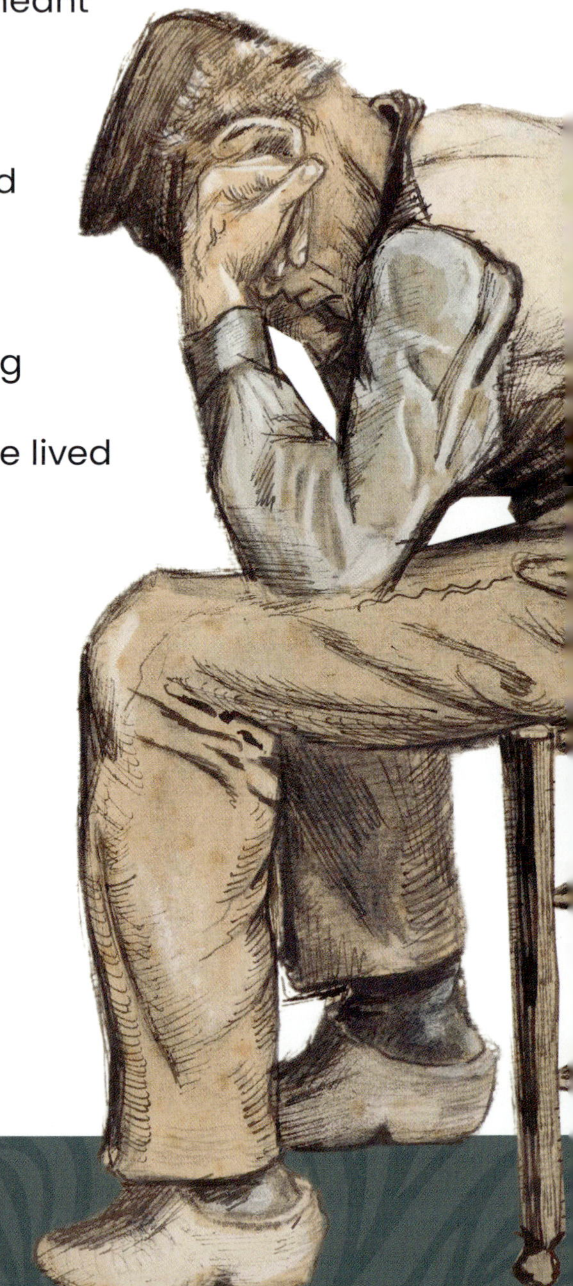

In 1881, Vincent returned to his

parents' home. Anton Mauve, a Dutch landscape painter, worked nearby in The Hague. He was a relative of the Van Goghs.

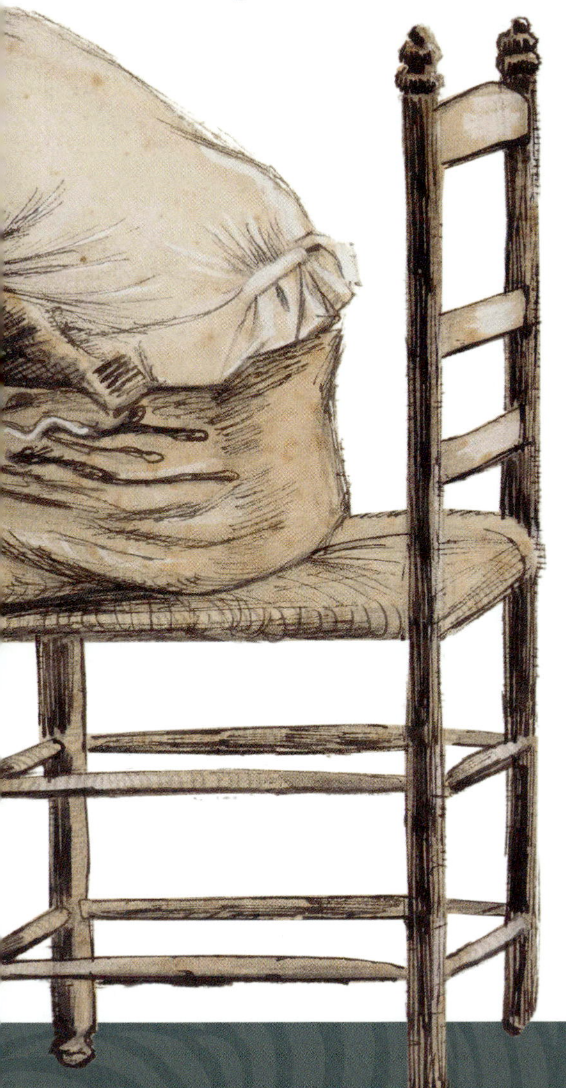

Vincent visited him often and learned from him. Mauve taught Vincent about watercolor and oils and gave him helpful **criticism** of his work.

Peasant Sitting by the Fireplace (Worn Out), *1881.*

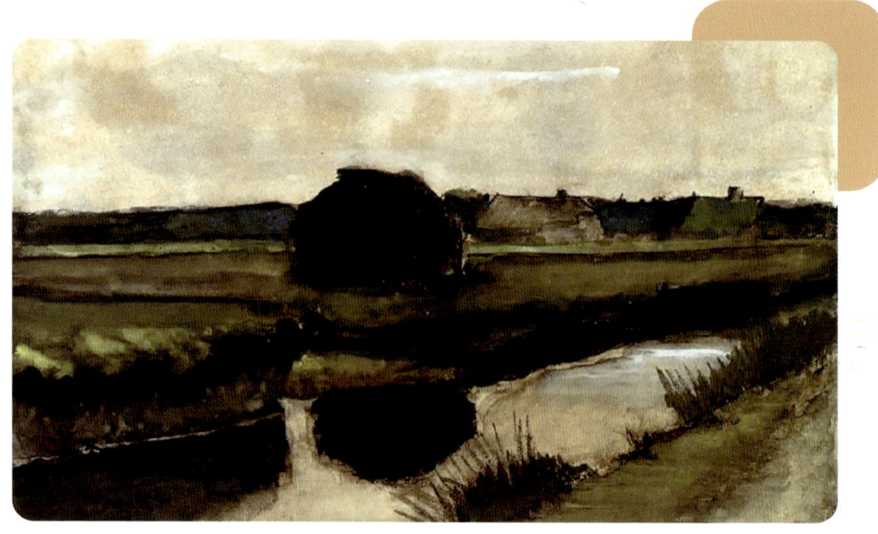

A watercolor of a Drenthe *landscape, 1883.*

Vincent moved to Drenthe in 1883 and put Mauve's lessons to use painting landscapes. While the area was peaceful, it was also lonely. He returned to live with his parents who now had a home in Nuenen. Vincent painted the weavers in the area. He focused again on capturing peasant life.

In 1884, Vincent painted a series of 40 peasant heads. These studies led to one of Van Gogh's early masterpieces, *The Potato Eaters* (1885).

Then, after a short stint studying art in Antwerp, Belgium, the ever-moving Vincent was ready for the City of Light.

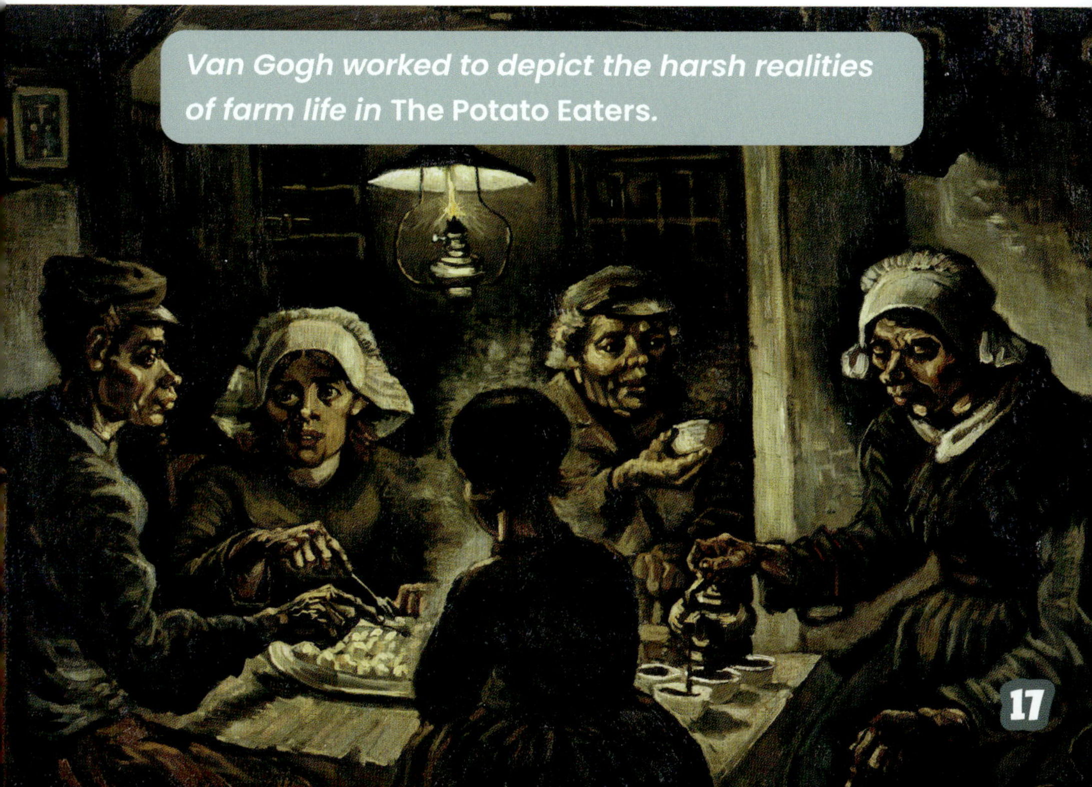

Van Gogh worked to depict the harsh realities of farm life in The Potato Eaters.

CHAPTER 3

POST-IMPRESSIONIST IN PARIS

Vincent had never seen **Impressionism** artwork before. His brother Theo tried to explain it through letters. But Vincent had to see it for himself in Paris. He liked the bright colors and the short, **expressive** brush strokes used by Impressionists.

Vincent began painting with more brilliant colors. And instead of just using

COMPLETE AN ACTIVITY HERE!

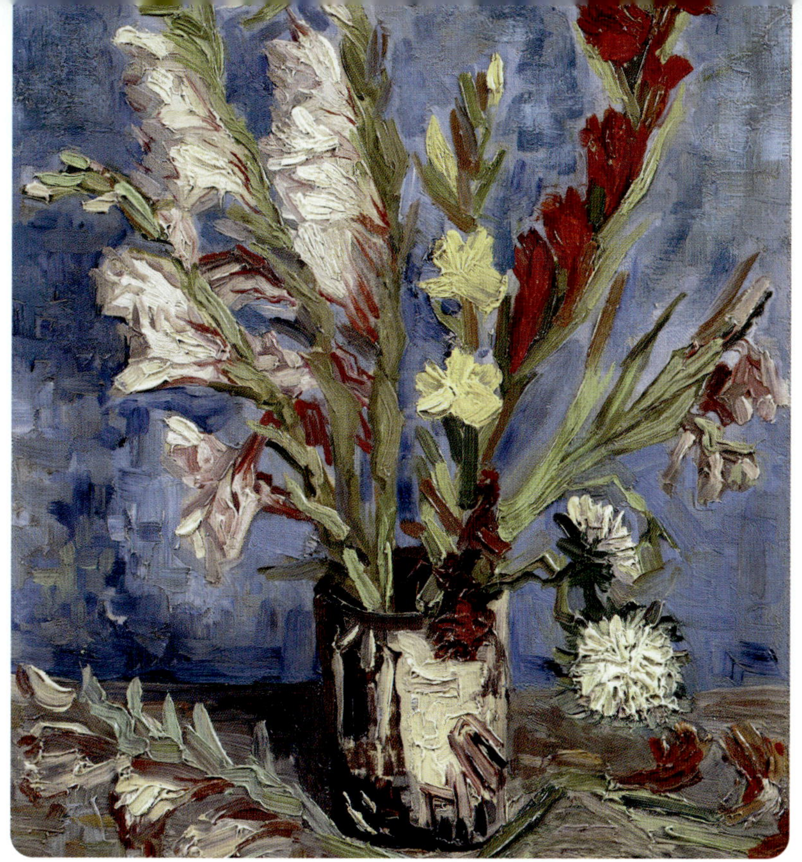

One of the more than 35 flower stills Van Gogh painted in Paris in the summer of 1886 while practicing his latest technique.

short brushstrokes, Vincent also painted short, bright lines of color. This became a well-known style later called Post-Impressionism.

WRITING ABOUT PAINTING

Today, 902 of Vincent's letters can be read. Most of them are to his brother Theo. The letters discuss Vincent's thoughts and ideas, as well as paintings he was working on or had completed. Many of the letters include sketches.

Paris was a great city for artists. Vincent made friends and organized art shows with them. He also painted more than 20 self-portraits.

But Vincent longed for a slower pace. In February of 1888, he moved to Arles, a city in southern France near the Mediterranean Sea.

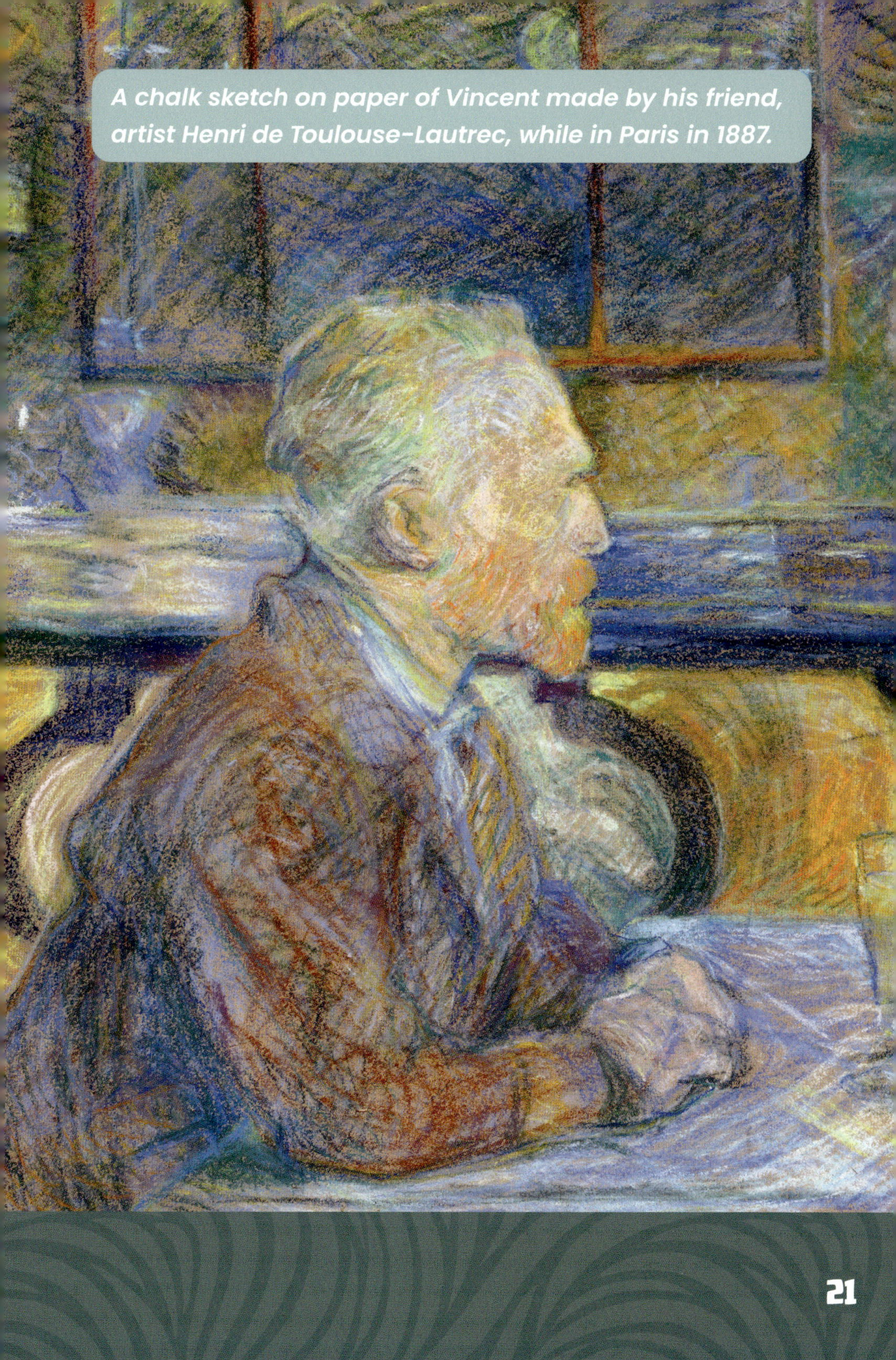

A chalk sketch on paper of Vincent made by his friend, artist Henri de Toulouse-Lautrec, while in Paris in 1887.

CHAPTER 4

THE YELLOW HOUSE

The sunshine and colors of Arles delighted Vincent. He got to work right away in his studio called the "Yellow House."

Vincent's style became looser and more **expressive** in his new home. In fact, he painted two of his most famous works in Arles in 1888: *Café Terrace at Night* and *The Night Café*.

EXPLORE LINKS HERE!

Soon after, artist Paul Gauguin came to live and work at the Yellow House. The men got along for the most part. But they had very different views on art. This led to heated arguments. After one of these fights, Vincent performed one of his most famous acts. On December 24, 1888, he cut off part of his left ear and spent two weeks in a hospital.

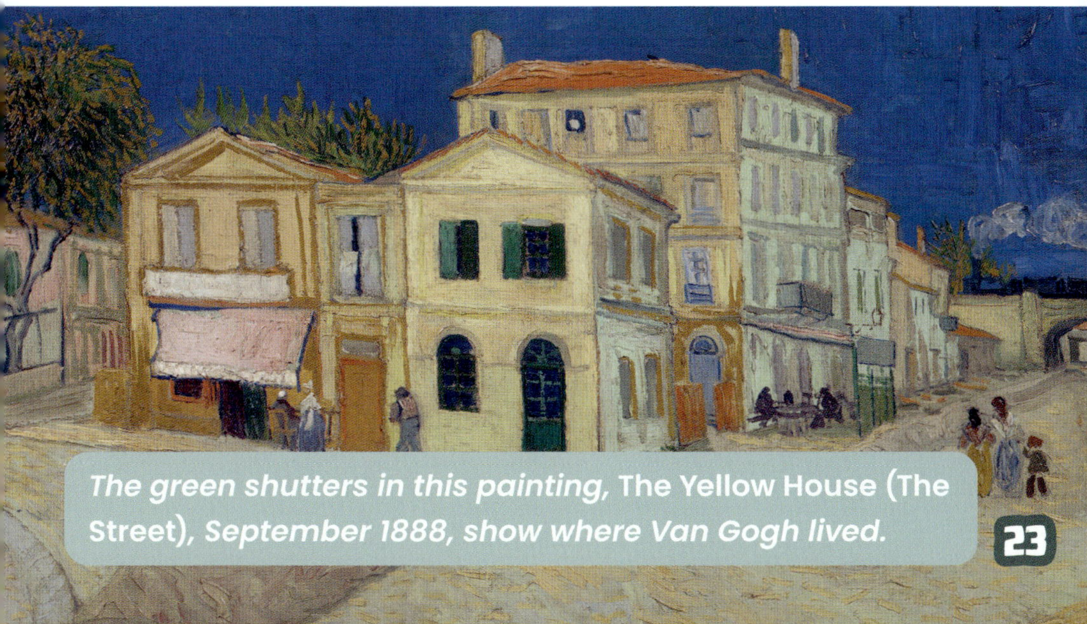

The green shutters in this painting, The Yellow House (The Street), *September 1888, show where Van Gogh lived.*

CHAPTER 5

PAINTING STARS AND BECOMING A STAR

Vincent went to a **psychiatric hospital** in January of 1889. During the day, he could venture out to paint flowers and trees. But he had to be back before nightfall. Because of this, Vincent painted night scenes by memory, including his celebrated *The Starry Night*. Theo, and

"It often seems to me that the night is much more alive and richly colored than the day."

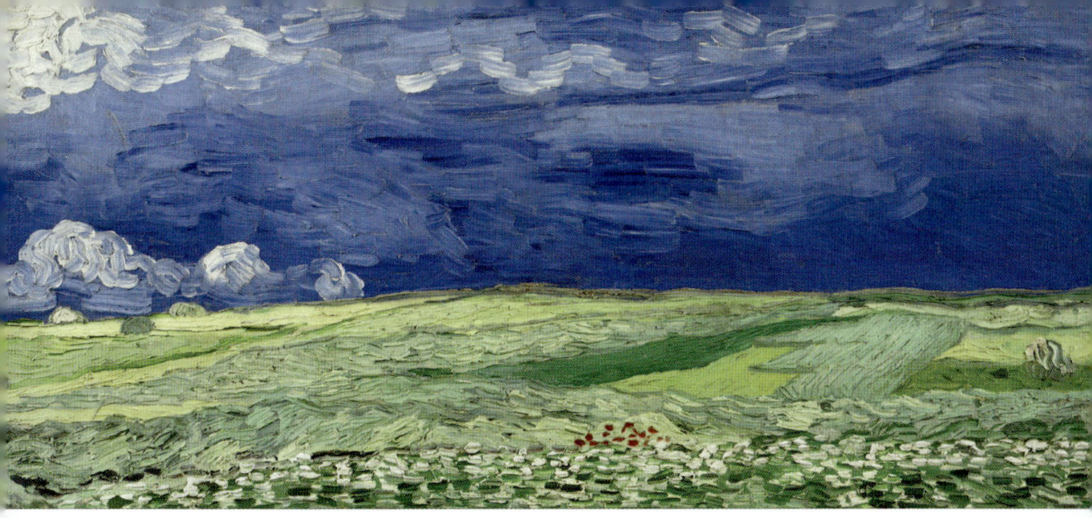

In a letter to Theo, Van Gogh wrote that he wanted to express "sadness, extreme loneliness" in Wheatfield under Thunderclouds *(1890).*

later critics, believed that Van Gogh's paintings during this time were his most beautiful.

Under the care of a doctor, Vincent was told to focus on art. He completed a painting a day. But his mental illness overcame him. Vincent van Gogh died on July 29, 1890, from a self-inflicted wound.

Theo died six months after Vincent. His widow, Johanna van Gogh-Bonger, loaned Vincent's paintings to museums. Buyers soon took notice of the artist's work. After Johanna's death, the collection was passed to her son. In 1930, he loaned the paintings to a museum in

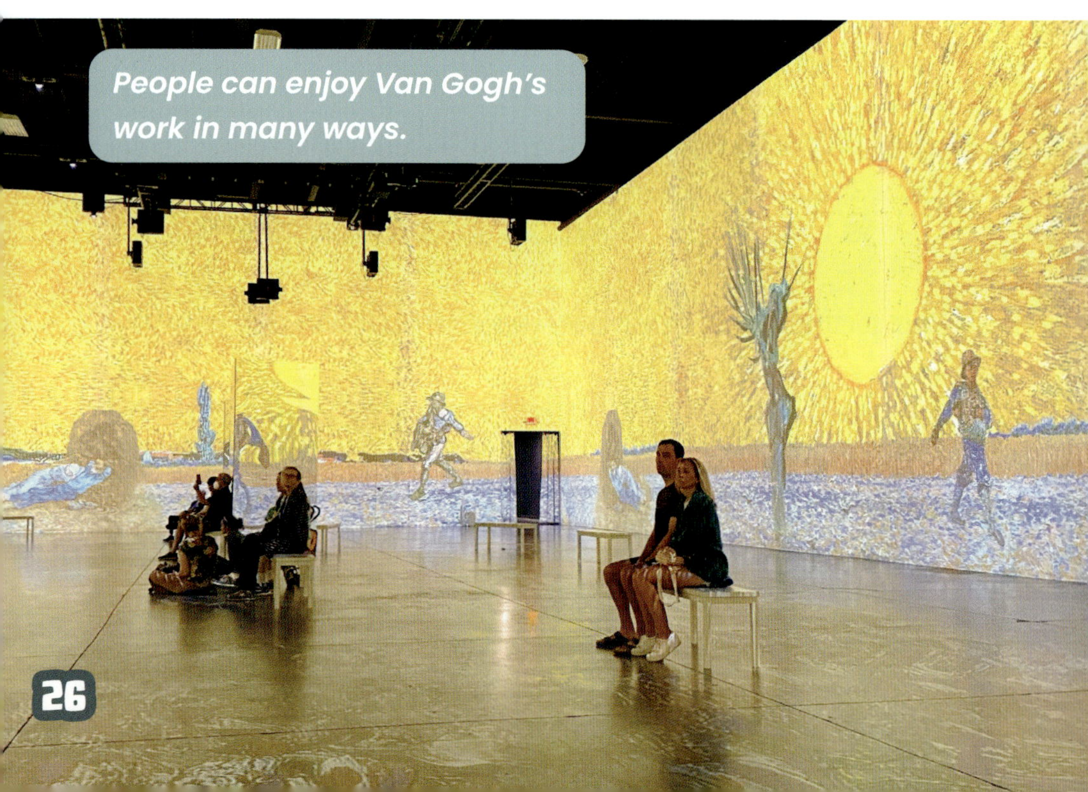

People can enjoy Van Gogh's work in many ways.

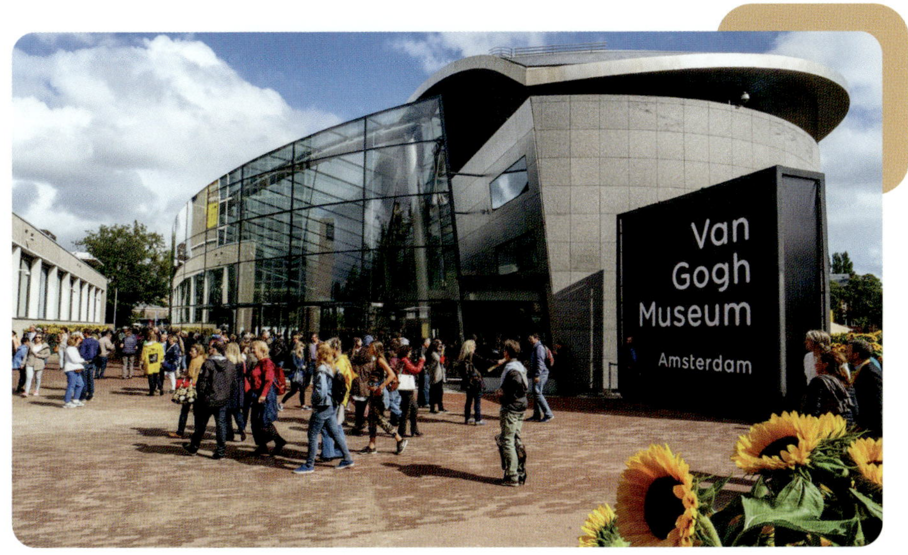

In 1991, 20 paintings were stolen from the museum but were soon recovered.

Amsterdam. It was there that Vincent's fame flourished.

In 1973, the Van Gogh Museum opened in Amsterdam. It holds the largest collection of Van Gogh's drawings and paintings. Due to the efforts of his family, the entire world knows the works of artist Vincent van Gogh.

IMPORTANT DATES

MARCH 30, 1853
Vincent van Gogh is born in Zundert, the Netherlands.

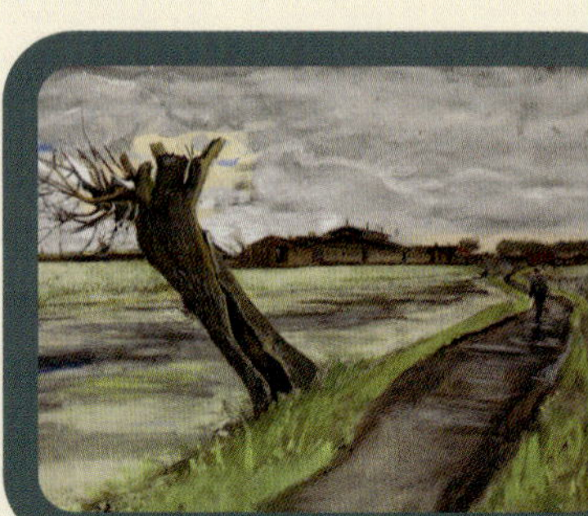

1881
Vincent learns about watercolor and oils from Anton Mauve.

1878
Vincent moves to Belgium's Borinage for 10 months as a missionary. His experience there begins his life as an artist.

1884-1885
Vincent paints a series of peasant heads. His unique style begins to shine through.

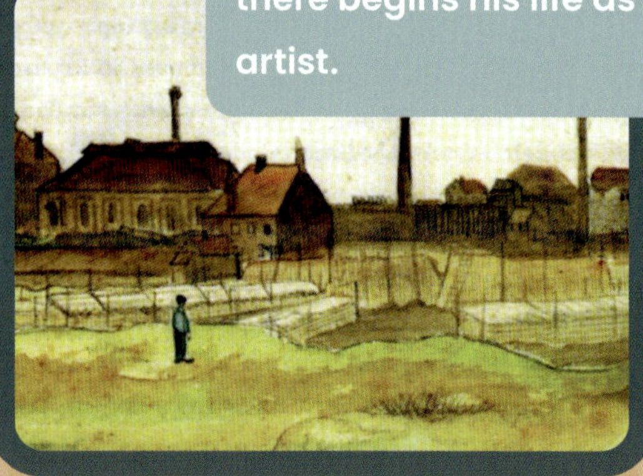

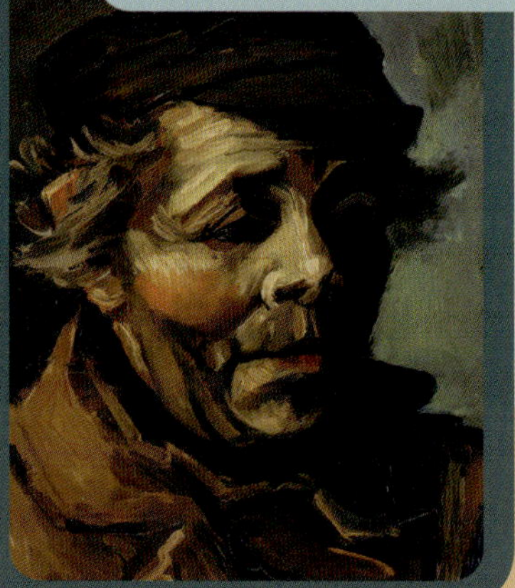

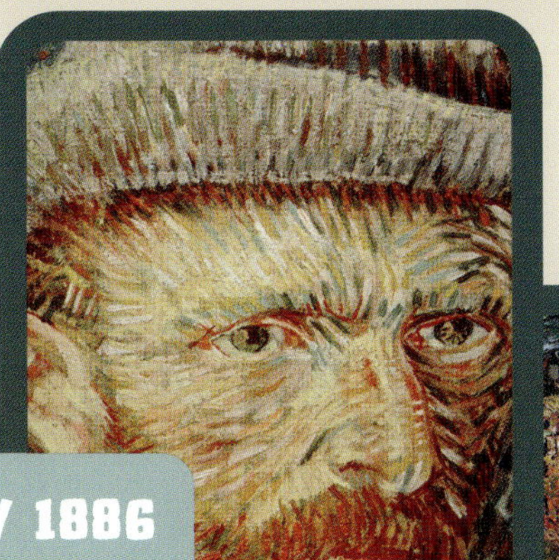

FEBRUARY 1886

Vincent moves to Paris where he begins painting with brighter colors. There, he paints more than 20 self-portraits.

JULY 29, 1890

Vincent dies at 37 years old after having sold just one painting in his lifetime (*The Red Vineyard*, 1888).

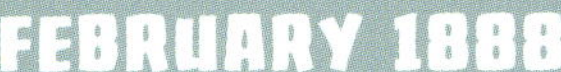

FEBRUARY 1888

Vincent moves to Arles where he paints two of his most famous works, *Café Terrace at Night* and *The Night Café*.

JUNE 2, 1973

The Van Gogh Museum opens in Amsterdam.

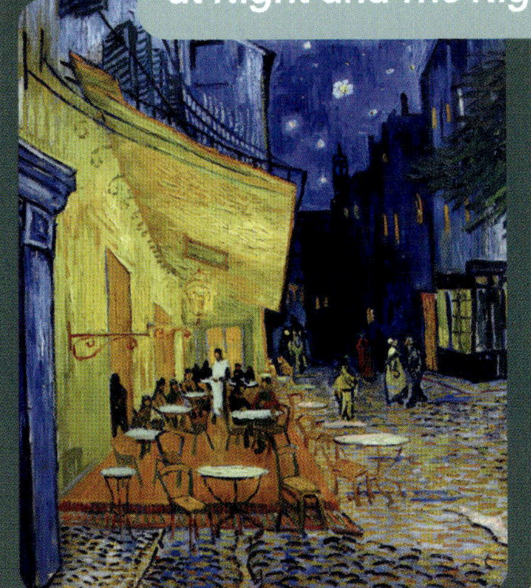

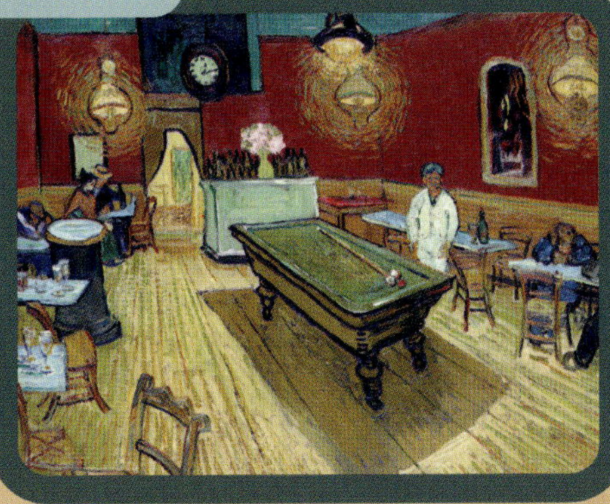

MAKING CONNECTIONS

TEXT-TO-SELF

What is your favorite work of art featured in this book? Explain why. How do you think Van Gogh was feeling when he painted it?

TEXT-TO-TEXT

Have you read any other books about an artist? How was their life similar to or different from Van Gogh's?

TEXT-TO-WORLD

Why do you think Van Gogh's artwork is so popular around the world? Do you believe art has an emotional effect on people?

GLOSSARY

apprenticed — placed as an apprentice to. An apprentice is someone who works for somebody else to learn a skill or trade.

criticism — the act of judging what is good or bad in something. A critic is a person who does the judging.

cultural — relating to something that promotes culture and arts.

expressive — full of feeling or meaning.

honing — perfecting.

Impressionism — a style of painting, originating in France in the late 19th century, directed toward capturing the life of a subject through observing the play of colored light and shadow upon it and painting quickly, using short brush strokes and unmixed colors.

missionary — a person who is sent by a church or religious order to another place to convert, heal, serve, or teach others about a certain religion.

peasant — a member of the class of farm workers and small farmers in Europe.

psychiatric hospital — an institution where patients with significant mental illnesses live while receiving treatment.

INDEX

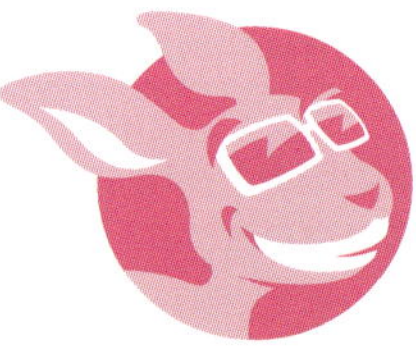

DiscoverRoo!
ONLINE RESOURCES

This book is filled with videos, puzzles, games, and more! Scan the QR codes* while you read, or visit the website below to make this book pop.

popbooksonline.com/van-gogh

*Scanning QR codes requires a web-enabled smart device with a QR code reader app and a camera.